Twisty and True Tails of a Shelter Dog Matchmaker

Twisty and True Tails of a Shelter Dog Matchmaker

JEAN M. ALFIERI

Published by Vintage Pups Publishing

ISBN (paperback): 979-8-9896976-0-1
ISBN (ebook): 979-8-9896976-1-8

Illustrations by Alexandra Ruiz
Book design and production by www.AuthorSuccess.com

Unless otherwise indicated all Scripture quotations are taken from The New King James Version of the Bible. Copyright 1979, 1980, 1982 by Thomas Nelson, Inc.

Dedication

To all dogs, and their many splendid personalities, that bring love, laughter, peace, and comfort into our otherwise hectic lives.

Contents

Foreword

Having worked in animal welfare for almost thirty years, these stories really resonated with me.

I am all too familiar with the sad souls, like Sweet Lady Jane, who have found their way to our shelter. More times than I can remember I have looked into the eyes of those senior pets, wondering what their story is and wishing they could tell me.

The story of Dean made me laugh. The little dog with the big voice was fantastic. I could feel his anguish over being alone and then his relief after being picked up and held.

I shed several happy tears reading this wonderful short story collection that highlights the commitment, love, and sacrifice of working with shelter pets. It makes a great gift for anyone who has adopted a pet, or has donated to, worked in, or volunteered at an animal shelter.

In three words, this book is humorous, insightful, and heartwarming.

~Jamie Norris, Director of Animal Law Enforcement, Humane Society of the Pikes Peak Region

Introduction

Get the Ball!

If only all our biggest challenges could be so simple. Navigating life takes wisdom, grace, and patience. None of these qualities I can claim in great abundance. But I've learned some critical lessons in these areas from my work at the Humane Society of the Pikes Peak Region, as a volunteer matchmaker and transport partner and then as a member of the administrative staff.

I have also been blessed to be a fur-mom to more than a dozen senior "rescue dogs,"—dogs that my husband and I have adopted from a shelter rather than purchased from a breeder or pet store. We prefer to call them "vintage puppies," and we've joked that if they don't need arthritis medication or supplements, we're not interested in being their steward!

This book is a combination of stories from the Humane Society and from home that display how a dog's faithful companionship is truly a gift from God. In it, you will meet a variety of canine characters, each of which had an impact and an important life lesson to offer. You'll enjoy original pictures, special quotes, inspiring scripture, and paw-some thoughts.

There is also a special treat at the end: a bonus back story on "the biggest dog in the house," and a confession. Nothing scandalous, but rather a glimpse of what I have learned about volunteering — something life in the 'corporate world' will never teach you.

Step into each short story and delight in the special bond we share with dogs. You may even be reminded of your own wonderful fur-family memories and the life lessons they've taught you. Let's go!

Inspiring Quote:

Dogs come into our
lives to teach us about
love. They depart to
teach us about loss.
A new dog never
replaces an old dog,
it merely expands
the heart.

-ERICA JONG

Rover, Who Was All Over

(Finding Our Way)

You know what I like
about people?
Their dogs.
~ UNKNOWN

The Humane Society is a popular place on Friday afternoons, so I wasn't surprised when there were six parties still waiting their turn, as notification came over the speakers that visitation would be ending in twenty minutes. As a "matchmaker," it was my job to facilitate meetings on a first come, first served basis. The commitment to adopt is determined during these visits, so we don't rush them.

The announcement prompted Sue to come over. She introduced herself when she arrived a little past 3 p.m. and had waited patiently since then. She had driven two hours for a dog she had seen on our website. Since she was still there, I assumed the dog she wanted to meet hadn't yet been adopted.

"Will we still get to see our dog?" her voice trembled with concern.

After driving that far and waiting that long, I would be concerned too.

"Yes," I assured her, "You are next in line so someone will be with you shortly."

"Great," she sighed, "We don't want to leave without him."

Interesting comment, I thought. Often people keep an open mind about whether a meeting will result in adoption. It sounded like she had already made up her mind. When we had spoken earlier, I thought she was alone. This time I noticed the man who stood behind her. He was tall with a thick build, cropped hair, no facial expression, and he did not say a word. I would have been intimidated if I didn't know my fair share of military and policemen. I looked at the emblem on his black shirt: El Paso County Police Department.

"Just hang in there," I offered.

They both nodded and returned to the bench where they'd spent the better part of the afternoon.

Dogs had been flying out the door. Which one were they so fond of that hadn't yet been picked? I did a quick sweep of the visitation room to ensure it was clean and grabbed some dog biscuits in case the next canine needed coaxing. I checked the waitlist and waved Sue over.

"It's your turn," I said smiling, "Who would you like to meet?"

She introduced her husband, Jim, and said, "We want to meet Rover."

My heart sank.

I was briefed on Rover when I arrived and his notes were clear: Rover pulls on leash, likes to jump, is mouthy, and plays aggressively. I had been candid with others who inquired about him that afternoon. I didn't want to steer them away but had to make sure they understood what they might be getting into.

I pulled Rover's information up on the computer and saw some additional notes about earlier visits. None had resulted in adoption. I worried this would be another failed attempt at a match.

"Let me tell you what I can about Rover."

Jim stepped forward so he could hear.

"He's a nine-month-old German Shepard mix. He has a ton of energy. He likes to pounce and play rather aggressively. He's eighty pounds and not yet at his full height or weight. He can become mischievous if not exercised frequently. He's mouthy and chews on everything. In short, he is a lot of dog."

Earlier in the day, this had been sufficient detail to deter a new mom with an infant tucked on her hip, as well as an elderly gentleman, walking with a cane. But Jim just nodded.

"Sounds like a nine-month-old German Shephard," he said.

"You're familiar with the breed?"

"My current police partner is a German Shephard."

My heart skipped a beat. Could this be the family that Rover had been waiting for?

He continued, "They are working dogs. They need a purpose. If you don't give them a purpose and encourage them to use their senses and their muscle, they become bored and can get themselves into trouble."

I nodded and continued reading Rover's information.

"It says here that his previous owner, who surrendered him to the shelter, was in the military and got reassigned. He understands commands issued in German."

"No problem," said Jim.

"Alright. Let me show you to the visitation room. Here are some treats."

"I'd like to meet him first. Then if it's okay, I'll invite Sue in."

I got the officer settled in the room and grabbed a leash to retrieve Rover.

"Hello handsome," I said to Rover.

He jumped up on the kennel door and towered over me, his hot breath fanning my hair. Not yet at full height or weight? Yikes! This beast looked all German Shepard but was massive! I coaxed him down.

"Hang on big guy. You need to be on your best behavior. You may be meeting your new forever family."

Rover panted and stepped back to let me open the door. As soon as I had the collar on him, he barreled past me and took off, charging down the aisle. Grasping the leash with both hands I futilely shouted "WHOA!" and leaned back, putting all my weight in my heels. I was in for a ride, sliding past kennels, trying to steer him sled-dog style, until he finally slowed when we reached the corner.

I skidded to a halt and paused to catch my breath. We turned left and were at the door. I opened it a couple inches and tried to tell Jim I did not have this situation under control, but Rover knocked me aside and burst into the room.

Jim stood up, snapped his fingers three times, and pointed to the floor. Rover abruptly sat down and looked up at him with rapt attention. My mouth dropped in awe. Seriously? It was that simple?! Jim snapped his fingers again and pointed to the floor. Rover laid down.

Jim took a knee to pet Rover's head, and Rover promptly rolled over, chuffing with excitement, and wiggling on his back. Jim gently rubbed his chest.

It had to be a record—in less than thirty seconds, I knew this was a match.

"Should I invite Sue in?" I asked.

"Sure," said Jim. This was the first time I saw him smile.

As I walked the paperwork to the adoption desk, I smiled too. How incredible for Rover to be appreciated and allowed to be just how the good Lord made him. There can be nothing better (for a dog or a person) than to discover your purpose and be encouraged to use all of your unique gifts.

Officer Jim and his wife left a half-hour later with a new fur family member. Rover walked proudly and properly next to his new humans. Such a joyful day for them, and for me. For God to allow me to be the bridge that introduced this family to Rover was such a blessing. I got to witness the invitation and the expressions, both human and canine, of this perfect match.

Paw-some Thought:

We are born into a family of people. When we adopt, we choose that member to live and grow with us; to be a part of our family history. But when it comes to dogs, do we pick them—or do they pick us?

Inspiring Quote:

Coming together is the beginning. Keeping together is progress. Working together is success.

~ HENRY FORD

Bible Verse:

For as we have many
members in one body,
but all the members do
not have the same
function, so we, *being*
many, are one body
in Christ, and individually
members of one another.

Romans 12:4-5

Crazy Dog Mom

(Why We Care)

People think I'm crazy because
I talk to my dogs. What am I
supposed to do? Just ignore them
when they ask me a question?

~ UNKNOWN

I have probably been "that" dog mom for a while now, but my obsession became evident recently, when I took the precious Princess Zoey to the vet for a routine visit. Because she's blind, she needs to be steered or she'll walk into walls, off sidewalks and curbs ... you get the picture.

Sometimes it's easier just to pick her up. I only do that sometimes, since this beautiful bull-pug is not at all petite. Pugs usually weigh about twelve pounds, give or take. Zoey really took after the 'bull' in her bloodline, weighing in at twenty-six pounds and not an ounce overweight. (She is my little brick house.)

We zig-zagged our way into the vet clinic and after a short wait in the lobby, I hefted Zoey into my arms and the vet tech led us to a room.

"How is our pug princess doing?" the vet asked as she entered.

"Well, last time we were here you looked at this growth on her stomach. You said it was a mole, nothing to worry about. But it's gotten considerably bigger in the last couple months."

I struggled to flip Zoey over so the vet could see.

"I understand that at twelve years old, vintage pups get lumps, moles, skin tags, etc. I just want to be sure it isn't more serious."

"It still looks fine," the vet announced, "Just a mole."

"Should I have it removed? I mean, if this was a boy dog, I wouldn't bother, because I'm sure a boy dog wouldn't care. But Zoey is a princess after all, and this seems a bit unsightly—a monster mole on her belly. Being a girl dog, she would probably want it removed, right?"

The vet gave me a blank stare. I realized a second too late how ridiculous I sounded . . . and gave an embarrassed giggle. There was an awkward silence in which I felt my face turn three shades of red.

". . . Or maybe not," I offered.

"I don't think she minds," the vet said matter-of-factly. "We don't need to remove it unless YOU want to."

I knew she was right, and I'm glad my vet spoke frankly. But my self-talk still said my mini-royal should be able to go through life without a blemish. Maybe it's a crazy dog-mom thing. But, regardless of species, if we don't care for (and about) each other, who will?

Inspiring Quote:

To make a difference
in someone's life
you don't have to
be brilliant, rich,
beautiful, or perfect.
You just have to care.

~ MANDY HALE

Bible Verse:

And be kind to one
another, tender-hearted,
forgiving each other,
even as God in
Christ forgave you

~ EPHESIANS 4:32

A Match for Frenchie

(Celebrate Others)

Everyone thinks they have the best dog, and none of them are wrong.

~ W. R. PURCHE

Ever been involved in a story so good, though your part in it is completely insignificant, you cannot help but tell it? This is that story.

I started my weekly shift as doggy matchmaker (introducing people to their choice of stray or surrendered pups). It was slow so I perused the list of available pets. My eyes stopped at the description of a three-year-old male French bulldog mix, who was being held for medical treatment. This dog was neither a stray nor surrendered but had been transferred from another state, severely underweight, and there were some vague notes that hinted at neglect. Since he was not up for adoption, he wasn't in our section of dogs. I went over to my fellow matchmaker, John, who having volunteered for over two years (versus my three months), was a wealth of information.

"Hey, John. Have you seen this male Frenchie-mix in the system?"

"Not in person. I heard he's cute."

"I've always wanted a Frenchie," I whispered, as if my husband were standing there. Josh would not be thrilled with the idea of a fourth dog.

"Wanna go take a look at him?" John asked.

Of course, I did!

When our shift ended, we walked back to the medical area. A much-too-skinny, black-and-white little French bulldog cowered at the back of his kennel. It was okay to give him treats and I had some hotdog slices ready. The smell brought him to me.

"Hi Sweetie," I cooed as he gobbled them up.

He drooled everywhere. Then sneezed. Snot went flying.

"Ewww. You're a messy one, huh?"

But nothing could taint his perfection. I was in love!

Before leaving for the day, I stopped at the front desk and put a 'choice hold' on the little Frenchie. That meant, as soon as he was cleared from his medical hold, I would be able to adopt him.

I drove home strategizing how to best break the news of our pending new addition to Josh. I decided to dispense the details slowly. I explained what little I knew of the neglect, how handsome he was, a little bit about his sneezing and drooling, and more about how handsome he was, so that fact was clear.

"He sounds cute, but kind of slobbery," said Josh.

"Oh, so slobbery," I smiled in agreement.

Josh tilted his head, figuring it out, "You want to adopt him, don't you?"

"THAT is a great idea!"

Josh did not share my zeal for a fourth pup and in the end, I conceded. I called and cancelled my choice hold, but even though I was not going to take him home, I wanted to keep track of what happened with the Frenchie.

When I went back the following week, he was five days away from being released. He'd been moved to the public section of kennels but could not yet receive visitors. I walked over to see him and there was a guy, sitting on the floor on the other side of the glass outside his kennel. As I came closer, I heard the guy talking to the Frenchie. He was telling him about his neighbors and how close the nearest dog park was to his place. I chuckled, thinking it a bit odd. Then I saw the dog. He had filled out so well. His ribs no longer showed. He stood taller and was right up at the front of the kennel, wagging his tail. The two never took their eyes off each other.

I walked over to John.

"Who's the guy talking to my Frenchie?"

"That's Bob. He's got a 'choice hold' on your Frenchie. And Bob has named him Butch."

"Butch is a great name for him!"

"Bob works across the street. I see him every Wednesday, browsing the kennels. But I've never seen him take such an interest in a dog. Now he shows up every day during his lunch to visit Butch. I have overheard some of the conversations. He tells Butch about how many days are left until he can go home and how he's bought him a nice new bed. Another day he talked about the side-by-side food and water bowl he found at Goodwill. Bob spends about a half-hour here and then goes back to work."

"He certainly sounds smitten! That is awesome."

"Yep. He even brought Butch a squeaky toy."

How perfect! Butch had found his best fur-ever home. John later told me when Bob finally met the little Frenchie in the adoption area, Butch jumped straight into his arms.

Nothing says 'happily ever after' quite like that!

Paw-some Thought:

Could this be what going to our heavenly home will be like? Butch's journey was a turbulent one, but he eventually landed in a loving forever home. I pray for God's mercy and grace so that like Butch, when my turbulent days are done, I will land softly in the loving arms of our Heavenly Father.

Inspiring Quote:

Scratch a dog and you'll find a permanent job.

~ Franklin P. Jones

Bible Verses:

Delight yourself also in
the Lord, and He shall give
you the desires of your heart.

Psalm 37:4

These things I have spoken to you,
that in Me you may have peace.
In the world you will have
tribulation; but be of good cheer,
I have overcome the world."

John 16:33

Epic Adoption Failure

(When Life Isn't Fair)

My fashion philosophy is,
if you're not covered in dog hair,
your life is empty.

~Elayne Boosler

"Is he housetrained?"

"I don't know if he's housetrained, how he became a stray, or why he stinks so bad."

Josh's frown deepened as he took another bite of his bagel, "What name did you decide on?"

"Mister Magoo."

This got a chuckle.

"He looks like a Magoo." Josh gave me a kiss and left for work, not-yet convinced this adoption was a good idea.

I, on the other hand, was thrilled to add to our pack. I was captivated by a two-year-old pug that had come into the shelter the week before. I prayed for him and hoped he would join our family. Today it was coming true. In a few hours, he would become ours.

I barely got his leash on before he bolted out of the kennel and chugged down the hall.

"Wow, you are sure rambunctious considering you just had surgery."

"Pant-pant-snort," was his reply.

"Okay," I planned out loud, "Let's get home, meet everyone, and then you'll relax."

The sounds of a panting pug and the stench of a stray dog filled my car.

The introductions went well. When our three older dogs realized they couldn't keep up with Magoo's frantic exploration of the backyard, they retreated inside. It was dinnertime, and as interesting as the new stinky guy was, they had their priorities.

Magoo raced into the house, jumped on and off the couch, dashed out to the yard and then back inside to repeat the course. During one intermission, he recklessly flipped the toy basket and in under two minutes had strewn a couple dozen stuffed plushies, tug-toys, and squeakies throughout the house, then circled back for more. His pant-snorting echoed off the walls.

"He's a swirling dervish," I muttered.

"Is he going to have a stroke?" Josh asked.

I wondered the same. The senior dogs that we usually adopt stroll into the house, select one of the assorted comfy dog beds, circle once or twice, and then lay down with a satisfied groan.

They look at us with big thankful eyes that say, "Wake me when it's mealtime," and life moves on.

This young one was a different story. By midnight Josh and I were exhausted. The other dogs had long since retired to their beds, giving us a "good luck," expression as they departed. I sat on the floor, hoping Magoo would come over, sit in my lap, and relax. No such luck.

My heart was desperate for this adoption to work out, but it didn't. I brought him back the next day and cried all the way home. I wondered, was I over-tired? Or relieved? Or was I truly disappointed this didn't work?

The more I thought about it, I realized that: maybe—just maybe—Magoo needed a place to be for only one more night so his forever family would find him. And our house was that place. When we pray for God to do His will and open our hearts to whatever He has designed for us, we can't then be disappointed when He does. We can be sad that it did not work out like we wanted, but we can also be delighted that we got to be part of that plan.

Though my heart was broken, I know it worked out as it was supposed to—and for that I am joyful.

P.S. Magoo was adopted within a half-hour of his return to the shelter.

Paw-some Thought:

Is there anything
you have been worried
or broken hearted over
that you can turn over to
God and trust it will turn
out just as it's supposed to?

Inspiring Quote:

You may encounter many defeats,
but you must not be defeated.
In fact, it may be necessary to
encounter the defeats, so you
can know who you are, what
you can rise from, how you
can still come out of it.

~ MAYA ANGELOU

Bible Verse:

For I know the thoughts
that I think toward you,
says the Lord, thoughts of
peace and not of evil, to give
you a future and a hope

Jeremiah 29:11

Sweet Lady Jane

(Comfort and Companionship)

The bond with a dog is
as lasting as the ties
of this earth can ever be.

~ KONRAD LORENZ

The best therapists
have fur and four legs.

~ UNKNOWN

It was an unusually slow day at the Humane Society. I was working as a "matchmaker" but the few people mingling around hadn't yet picked out a pup to visit, so I scrolled through the list of dogs on the computer.

A guy approached and asked, "Could I meet Lady?"

"Sure." I pulled up her profile.

"I don't want to adopt her, but she looks like such a sad, old dog, I thought I'd visit her."

Lady came up on my screen. She was absolutely a sad, old dog. It was against protocol to let people "just visit" because we are usually so busy. We want to focus on connecting those people who are ready to adopt and can leave with their new fur-family member. However, since it was slow (and I was a bit curious to meet her too), I figured making this exception would be fine.

The guy waited in the visitation room while I went to fetch Lady. I located her kennel and smiled. Once upon a time, she had a beautiful brindle coat which was now mostly grey. She stood awkwardly and her head was crooked, like she was riddled with arthritis.

"Hi there, pretty girl," I greeted her.

Her eyes met mine, but she did not even offer a tail wag. She seemed to doubt it was worth the expense of energy. But those eyes, like melted chocolate, were still clear and bright.

Lady hobbled along behind me on our way to the visitation room. Once inside, she stood, not making any move toward the guy. Nor did she pay any attention to me. I coaxed her over so we could both pet her head and admire her silky soft ears. She made no effort to connect. Lady showed no sign she was happy to be out of the kennel or to receive some love. Nothing. I thanked the visitor for taking the time to come in and returned Lady to her kennel.

It was still slow, so I read more on Lady's background. A boxer-beagle mix, she came in as a stray. It seemed unlikely she ran away. The poor thing could hardly walk. I hoped she would find a home soon. Senior dogs often struggle with getting adopted because people prefer younger dogs and puppies.

Much to my dismay, Lady was still there the following week when I arrived for my shift. This was unusual. At the time, most dogs were adopted out in a matter of days. I had not seen the same dog for two weeks in a row. I was hopeful when someone stepped up and wanted to meet her.

"She is really a lovely old soul," I offered.

"Well," said the young woman, "My friend asked me to come along. She's adopting a cat. While she's doing that, I thought I would visit a dog. Lady looks so sad and lonely, but I'm not going to adopt her or anything."

Hmph. I didn't bother explaining our protocol. Selfishly, I wanted to visit the old gal again. Maybe I could explain to Lady that she needed to up her enthusiasm a bit. A little tail wag would go a long way.

Nope. She shuffled along even slower this time. When she entered the visitation room, she plopped her butt on the floor, not even bothering to greet her visitor. The visitor came over and we both petted her. Her tail thumped once, and she sighed. I sighed too. This dog needed a home.

After my shift, over a bottle of wine, my husband, Josh, heard about Lady. We were down to two dogs at that point. He had lost his soul dog, an Airedale named Duke, whose personality superseded any other animal on the planet. He was a big boisterous beast, who would scramble to the door and march in place while eagerly waiting, whenever he heard the garage open, signaling Josh's return home. Duke never hid his affections, and our hearts were broken at his sudden passing. I knew it was too soon for Josh to consider another dog, but I had to try.

"We rescue vintage puppies," I said, "Lady is as vintage as they come. Would you at least drive over and meet her?"

"No," was his full response.

"I'm sad too. But if we wait until we're not sad anymore, we will never get another dog. You know that, right?"

"I'm not ready."

Like a good wife, I wouldn't let it go.

"She would fit right in here. You probably wouldn't even notice her around. Seriously. I think the best thing we could do is make her comfortable until she passes. I wonder if anyone's ever given her any attention. She does not belong stuck in a shelter."

"Fine. If she's still there when you go to work next week, you can get her. I'll meet you outside to help unload her when you get home."

Josh was banking on Lady getting adopted, but I let the topic rest.

Before leaving for my shift the following week, I went online to find her picture front and center, in the "Spotlight" section. I wasn't the only one to recognize how long she had been there. While three days was the typical adoption timeframe, she'd been waiting three weeks.

I went in a couple of hours early to complete the paperwork. When they brought Lady into the adoption lobby, she gave me one tail wag of recognition and sat down as if the walk from her kennel had taken all the gas she had.

We strolled slowly to my car, and it occurred to me that I wasn't sure how I would get her loaded in the back. She was fifty pounds; a bit more than I could dead lift. I opened the hatch of my Outback and we made eye contact.

"Here's the deal," I said, "If you can help me get you in here, there's someone at home that can help you out."

As I said, "Here we go!" and made a cradle for her, Lady gave a feeble jump which was just enough for me to catch and scoop her into the back. We were on our way.

I gave Josh a call when we were five minutes from home. He stood waiting for us in the drive. She was so frail we could not risk letting her jump out.

I parked and opened the hatch. Lady once again made a feeble leap . . . right into Josh's arms. In that instant she became the biggest 'daddy's girl' you'd ever meet. Her tail wagged whenever he entered the room. Wherever he sat, her head was on his lap. She would scrape herself off the floor to follow him around.

When Josh was away from the house, Lady thumped up the stairs to sleep alone. She never hung out with the riffraff—me and the other dogs! Though she did pick up some bad habits from the pug . . . like how to nuzzle and push for belly rubs, and how if she stared at the treat jar long enough, she might get one. She also learned the joy of squeaky toys.

We immediately got Lady on arthritis medication, and this dog, who I thought had only a few months left, gave us nearly two years of loving companionship in return. She could not have been more different from the big brute that was Duke, yet somehow filled a void that only her sweet, peaceful spirit could.

You can be sure this special old girl was very far from 'being sad' or 'lonely' as Josh sat with her on the floor and cradled her head as she crossed the rainbow bridge.

Paw-some Thought:

Sometimes, even when death has left a gaping hole in our hearts, we must trust God with our life. To be willing to accept even the smallest kindness to help us heal. Whether it be in the form of a short note, a phone call, or an old dog in need of a little love.

Inspiring Quote:

A dog is
one of the
few things
in life that is
exactly what
it seems.

~ Unknown

Bible Verse:

Blessed be the God and Father
of our Lord Jesus Christ,
the Father of mercies and
God of all comfort, who
comforts us in all our
tribulation, that we may
be able to comfort those
who are in any trouble,
with the comfort with
which we ourselves
are comforted by God.

2 Corinthians 1:3-4

The Littlest Things

(Praying for Ourselves)

You know you're a dog owner
when you can't go to the bathroom
without an escort.

~ UNKNOWN

I prayed before bed every night. There was a lot
to pray about. If I thought too much about it all, I
would lay awake worrying. A dear friend had recently lost her kitty companion of fifteen years and
her heart was shattered. Another friend was unex-
pectedly admitted to the hospital. She had gone to
urgent care the day before, where the doctors discovered a mass that might be cancerous. Yet another friend was struggling with seasonal depres-
sion. Christmas was looming. Wasn't this supposed
to be the most wonderful time of the year? To top it

off, my own family was struggling with some health issues.

I turned it all over to the Great Healer. As I drifted off to sleep, the one worry I kept in my heart was about my little Reggie, our fifteen-year-old chihuahua. As he aged, he'd become less tolerant of visits to the vet. We had discontinued his nail trimmings a couple of years before because he got so aggravated by his paws being touched that he would attack the tech. No harm was ever done (he is toothless and weighs only five pounds) but in his fits of rage, I worried that he would hurt himself.

I bought a sandpaper nail trimmer and we eased into a routine (including so many treats that he gained an extra pound). This was effective except for one nail—his right paw dew claw. I simply could not reach it from any angle without him trying to twist out of my grasp and becoming hostile. For two years I tried, and it had grown to the point of curling around and touching the pad. It had to be cut or it would start growing into his skin.

It weighed on me. Should I take him in to be sedated for a nail trim? It seemed an extreme and expensive measure for a simple nail clipping, but I had no other ideas.

The alarm on the clock next to my bed went off at five a.m. and as I reached over to turn it off, I heard a voice. The voice was not so much in my ears as it was in my heart.

It said, "Why don't you ask me for help with Reggie?"

I was startled. I was groggy. I tried to get my bearings, reaching down to pat Reggie who was snuggled by my hip.

"What?" I whispered. (Since I don't often hear ambient voices, I strongly suspected where this message was coming from.)

"Don't you think I can help you with Reggie?"

My heart pounded. Of course. I knew with complete confidence that God could help me with Reggie. My thoughts swirled. I hadn't included Reggie in my prayers because:

1. There were more important things for God to focus on, right? I had the list, and I had it prioritized!

2. I should be able to take care of Reggie. He is such a small responsibility (literally). Why should I bother God with Reggie's nail care?!

3. I worried about wasting God's time. He's busy. If I think I am busy (and I do) he must be going nonstop with all the special requests He is fielding!

That was as far as I got before I realized the silliness of my rationale. I paused and listened for the voice. Nothing. My heart was calm.

I sighed at my foolishness.

1. God could likely prioritize His list of important things very well without my assistance.

2. Even Reggie needed God's care and we are fortunate to have a God that loves all His creations and watches over all of us.

3. He is not concerned about time. He is never too busy. He loves when we talk to Him, no matter when or how trivial it may seem to us.

Before I got out of bed, I prayed over Reggie and asked that God give me the strength, ingenuity, and patience to trim that dew claw.

I was talking to a friend about it later that day and she mentioned a YouTube video she saw of someone dealing with an irritable dog who did not want his nails trimmed. The blessing of that casual chat gave me an idea.

I enlisted Josh's help. He stood in front of Reggie while I held him in my lap with the traditional nail clippers. As I twisted myself around to address the dew claw, Josh focused only on feeding Reggie a big spoon smeared with peanut butter. As he slobbered his way through it, I gently maneuvered his nail into place and CLIP! It was done—with only a minor growl from Reggie, whose attention quickly returned to the spoon. Hallelujah!

Paw-some Thought:

Have you asked Him for help?
Why not? Are you worried
about wasting His time?
Is it too insignificant?
If God cares about my
precious little drama-rama
chihuahua, He most certainly
cares about YOU.
Just ASK!

Inspiring Quote:

Any concern too small
to be turned into
a prayer is too small
to be made into
a burden.

~ Corrie Ten Boom

Bible Verse:

Be anxious for nothing,
but in everything by prayer
and supplication, with
thanksgiving, let your
requests be made known
to God; and the peace of God,
which surpasses all
understanding, will guard
your hearts and minds
through Christ Jesus.

PHILIPPIANS **4:6-7**

Missing My Co-pilot

(When Sadness Surfaces)

> You think dogs will not be in heaven? I tell you, they will be there long before any of us.
>
> ~ Robert Louis Stevenson

"Congratulations," he said as he dropped the new set of keys into my open hand.

"Thanks," I mumbled, "And congrats to you. You now have a great used car to sell."

I had traded in my six-year-old Outback for the newest model. For all my car-driving life, I've always owned a Subaru. It's been almost thirty years. I can't drag myself away from a company that consistently provides a solid, reliable vehicle and friendly, competent customer service.

So why couldn't I shake this feeling of melancholy?

I sat in the driver's seat and took deep breaths to relish that new car smell, then drove away from the dealership and tried to identify what was missing.

When I arrived home, my fifteen-year-old son stood in the garage and admired the new car at great length. He loved all the special features: the paddle shifters, the keyless entry, the reverse camera—none of which were on my previous Outback.

With great enthusiasm, Collin asked, "How do you like it?"

With a weak smile, I answered, "It's okay."

He looked at me wide-eyed, "It's got all these cool options! Why is it only 'okay'?"

I gave him a hug.

"It is a great car, with more features than I've ever had. But this car will never have the memory of a cute little, grey-muzzled pug sitting in my passenger seat, eager to get to the park."

He hugged me back.

"Then maybe it's time to make some new memories."

A vision flashed before me of how our family would use this new car: my son driving it next year to attend prom, weekend road trips with my husband, and possibly a new smooshy-faced little dog peeking out the passenger window. Collin was so right.

Paw-some Thought:

How long does one miss a beloved pet? Forever, I'll offer. It is nothing to be ashamed of. I adore the vintage puppies in our home and treasure the time we have with them. That does not mean I don't miss all the others— including this special pug. Cheers to Wyatt!

Inspiring Quote:

"There are no happy endings.
Endings are the saddest part,
So just give me a happy middle
And a very happy start."

~ Shel Silverstein

Bible Verse:

Blessed are those who mourn, for they shall be comforted.

Matthew 5:4

Durango Rescue Run

(Enjoy the Moments)

"Don't accept your dog's
admiration as conclusive
evidence that you
are wonderful."

~ ANN LANDERS

Priscilla and I hit the road early on a cold, snowy day in late January. It had been almost a year since the last Humane Society rescue run . . . when Covid shut everything down. I was excited to receive the call and to meet a new partner. The weather was no deterrent as we were both joyous to return to this fun and meaningful work. Finding much in common, there wasn't a single gap in our conversation during the eight-hour drive from Colorado Springs to Durango.

We checked into our rooms then grabbed dinner before retiring.

We checked out early the next morning and stepped out of the hotel into a bone-chilling four-degree swirling wind. To our dismay, both the sliding side door and the back door of our cargo van were frozen shut. We climbed into the cab and let the van warm up. We were scheduled to meet our first shelter partner right down the road, in an hour. We cranked up the heat in the back and were confident the doors would loosen by then. We stopped for coffee then parked at the first of five shelters at which we would pick up dogs along our route back.

Scott, driving the van bringing dogs from New Mexico, arrived promptly at eight a.m. Priscilla and I stepped out to meet him. He had ten dogs and nine puppies to unload. The kennels had been prepared the day before, so we were ready to start the transfer. I pulled firmly on the sliding door of the van. It didn't budge. Not even a little. I tugged some more. Nothing. I went around to the back. That door was still frozen, too. Priscilla tried. Scott tried. No luck.

We considered our very limited options. We got buckets of hot water from the shelter and poured them down the doors. It did not work and may have made matters worse. Getting it into a warm garage would have helped, but this was a huge cargo van. We needed a local hero. Someone with special talent . . . the fire department! I grabbed my phone and found the nearest station just ten minutes away. Scott agreed to wait, and we headed off.

I rang the doorbell of the firehouse and out stepped Hero #1. I explained our issue. He grabbed his coat and as we moved toward the vehicle, Hero #2 emerged. They conferred, inspected the van, and pulled on the sliding door. It didn't budge. Not even a little. Hero #1 walked to the back and pulled on that door. Shazam—it opened!

Running an hour behind schedule, this was good enough for us. Priscilla and I thanked the firemen and drove back to the shelter where Scott and nineteen dogs patiently waited. En route, we discussed our new strategy. Loading dogs from the back was possible, but not nearly as easy, given the three-foot step. It required that we hoist ourselves with the assistance of a pull-handle, which we could not do while maneuvering a dog in our arms. We agreed that Priscilla would be on the ground, handing the dogs up to me. I would stoop and receive them and put them in their respective kennels. This would take longer but was the safest option.

Back at the shelter, we tried the sliding door one more time. It was still frozen shut. Scott brought each dog around and told Priscilla their name. She relayed this to me so I knew in which kennel they should be placed. She started handing off dogs with a manner and efficiency that reminded me of . . . me! She was very succinct, checking off each dog on the list, handing them off and expediently moving on to the next.

I, on the other hand, felt a wave of . . . what was it? Not "compassion," though I feel that whenever I'm assigned to these runs. It is wonderful to rescue dogs, knowing this may be their only chance at life. I always pray it is not just any life they get, but the BEST life.

One of the pups rolled over in my arms and looked up with big brown eyes. This feeling was greater than compassion. It was a sense that even though we were running late, and we could make up time by moving quickly through this process, what we really needed to do was slow down. As Priscilla handed me the third of nine puppies, that is exactly what I did. I began welcoming each of them.

"Good morning, little cutie, how are you? You will be riding with your litter mates right here."

I received the next puppies:

"How are you doing this fine day? So glad you're here. We're in for a long drive, so settle in and get comfy."

Then the dogs:

"So happy to see you! We have been looking forward to meeting you. I'm Jean and this is Priscilla. We will be your escorts today."

"Hello Momma. Aren't you beautiful? You did a great job with these puppies!"

"Hello, Bubba. Ooh, aren't you a big hunk of love?"

I bent to give Bubba a scratch behind his ears and he rewarded me with a big tail wag. They all seemed to enjoy the special attention, and when Priscilla heard me greeting each dog, she chuckled and slowed down.

During our drive, we pondered this. How often do we rush past each other? If we could be as genuinely kind to our fellow humans as we were to these dogs; if we could forego our schedule for a few minutes to show compassion, consideration, and sincerely care about each other . . . wouldn't our neighborhood, our city, our world be a better place?

Paw-some Thought:

There is much to be said about due dates and timelines, but if we learned anything in 2020, it's that nothing is certain except our **love** and **respect** for one another. These dogs helped me realize that. It may have seemed like a routine trip on an otherwise non-descript winter day, but I emerged a different person. From now on, I am leading with my heart.

Inspiring Quote:

Before you get a dog you can't quite imagine what living with one might be like. Afterward, you can't imagine living any other way.

~ CAROLINE KNAPP

Bible Verses:

Let each of you look not only to his own interests, but also to the interests of others.

PHILIPPIANS 2:4

Therefore, comfort* each other and edify**each other, just as you are also doing.

1 THESSALONIANS 5:11

*Or encourage

** Build one another up

Screamin' Dean

(Transformation)

Dogs don't see the outside of a human but the inside of a human.

~ CESAR MILLAN

My transport-partner and I first learned about Dean as we drove the van to a neighboring shelter, where we were scheduled to pick up several dogs.

Our rescue roster was set. We knew who we would pick up and had their stations set up with comfy bedding for the ride. En route, I received a text from our transport manager:

"Could you please check on a 'screaming chihua-hua?' I have a description but cannot picture the screaming in my head so I'm not sure we'd be able to place him."

"Oh boy," I said to Larry and read him the text.

"Hmmm," was his response.

"I know. I love our chihuahua, but he can be a handful."

Larry and his wife are cat people, so I briefly described for him the little five-pound, fifteen-year-old, toothless terror we call Reggie.

"Why don't you go in and meet Dean," Larry said as he parked the van in front of the shelter.

I was greeted by Jenifer. We introduced ourselves and cut to the chase.

"Want to meet Dean?" she asked and started down the hall.

I jogged to catch up. We were at his kennel before he saw us approach. He was a wiggly little thing with a beautiful reddish coat and long body.

"Can I go in?" I asked Jenifer.

"Sure. He's super friendly."

He sure was. Dean brought me a ball, and when I sat down, he plopped right in my lap.

"You seem sweet enough," I said as he crawled up into my arms and kissed my cheek.

"Oh no," I warned him, "My husband made me promise I wouldn't come home with another dog."

Dean was not deterred. He continued snuggling.

Jenifer laughed, "I'm so glad you like him."

"What's his deal?"

"He does this screaming thing," she explained. "People just aren't interested in meeting him. He has been to two other shelters and I'm not sure we can adopt him out."

This seemed like an easy decision. I put Dean on a leash, and he walked right next to me. We met Larry outside and Dean obediently sat.

"We should take him," I said.

"Looks like it," Larry agreed.

He and Jenifer loaded up the other dogs and we made up a station for Dean. I set him inside and closed the door . . . and oh, the SCREAMING! It was not a loud bark or an obnoxious whine. It was a mind-blowing, blood-curdling, ear-piercingly abrasive scream.

Larry and I looked at each other in horror as I slammed the sliding door shut.

"Wow," was all I could muster.

"I guess that's the scream," he said, rubbing his left ear, "I hope it stops when we get moving."

It did. Dean was fine until we arrived at our next stop and the sliding door was opened. The shelter helpers covered their ears.

"Should I get Dean?" I shouted over the noise to Larry.

Before he could answer, the shelter helpers yelled in unison, "YES!"

I opened Dean's kennel and scooped him into my arms. He quieted immediately.

"Oh, this is how it's going to be," I said to him. He wagged his tail in response.

Dean and I watched as more dogs were loaded into the van. He was very satisfied to be a spectator and did not make a peep. But once he was loaded back into his station, the screaming resumed.

"He is going to need some clicker training before he's ready for adoption," I said, "Good thing we have a rock-star behavior team to help him."

"Yes," said Larry, "And good thing our next stop is home."

We discussed how to best manage Dean when we arrived at the shelter. To avoid upsetting the other dogs aboard, I hopped out and quickly re-trieved Dean from his station. Larry went to locate helpers to unload our cargo. This gave me a few minutes alone with Dean.

He was content in my arms, so I held him as we walked around the garage. I knew we had to address the elephant in the room. I deployed my best "positive feedback" training and launched into it.

"Dean," I started. He looked at me and sniffed my face. I had his attention. "You are in a very special place. This may be the best opportunity for you to find your forever home."

He licked my cheek. So far so good.

"We should talk about some techniques for getting adopted."

He crawled up to my shoulder and laid down his head. I whispered softly in his ear.

"You are super cute. But this screaming thing you do is not one of your most attractive qualities. The sooner you can manage that, the sooner your human will find you. God has something very special planned for you and that human. What do you think?"

Dean sighed and nestled into my neck.

"You're right," I replied to Dean, "It has been a long day. You are a good boy and you're going to be okay."

Dean was a quick study and got himself adopted less than two weeks later. After the many failed attempts to get him to the right place at the right time to be discovered by his forever-family. I'm glad we took the chance on him.

Paw-some Thought:

I see myself in Dean. Being the 'best version of me' is a daily challenge. And it does not get easier with age. I notice more shortcomings every year! I thank the Lord each day for His provision, and pray He guides me in all I think, say, and do.

Inspiring Quote:

Allow the fires of transformation to burn away all that doesn't serve you.

~ HEATHER ASH AMARA

Bible Verse:

And do not be conformed
to this world, but be transformed
by the renewing of your mind,
that you may prove what *is*
that good and acceptable
and perfect will of God.

ROMANS 12:2

Rumble all the Way

(Determination in Action)

Every morning you have two
choices: Continue to sleep with
your dreams or wake up
and chase them.

~ CARMELO ANTHONY

Sometimes you have to go back to the beginning. Allow me to introduce Rumble, brought home by my parents when I was seven years old—a very impressionable age to start learning life lessons taught by a dog.

Rumble liked to sleep on the sofa. On occasion, he allowed me to join him. Since Rum weighed more than me, I let him sleep wherever he wanted. Our dad did not feel the same way.

"He doesn't belong on the sofa," Dad said.

Ours was not a house in which you asked why. If you did, "Because I said so," was likely the answer. Rumble didn't ask—nor did he listen. It was soon a battle of wills. The bad habit had taken root and Dad took action.

To prevent Rumble from getting on the couch, Dad barricaded the sofa with chairs. The first time was rather funny, but an expression of despair clouded the big dog's face. He stood, staring at the upside-down chairs stacked in his favorite napping place. I encouraged him to lay on his blanket, but he would have none of it. I left him there, head tilted, calculating.

I returned from the kitchen, snack-in-hand, and almost dropped my plate when I saw what he'd done. Rumble had wiggled between the chairs and positioned his rump on the backside of one of them. It was completely awkward, but he wasn't done . . .

After he wedged himself atop the barricade, he slowly started to push. First one chair backward, then the other one forward, until he had just enough space in between to lay down. He did so with a loud grunt, expressing his displeasure at this new roadblock to comfort.

When Rumble heard the door from the garage open, indicating Dad's entrance, he slid stealthily to the floor and laid down in one seamless motion. Dad passed through the living room without even glancing in his direction. Score one for the dog!

Rumble didn't always win though. As he got older it became harder to make that masterful move off the sofa before being caught by Dad. But he did not give up; he got smarter. When that beautiful beast realized he couldn't physically haul himself up and off the sofa before Dad walked from the garage through the living room, he simply sat still. It went like this:

- Rumble would be enjoying an afternoon nap between the chairs on the forbidden couch.

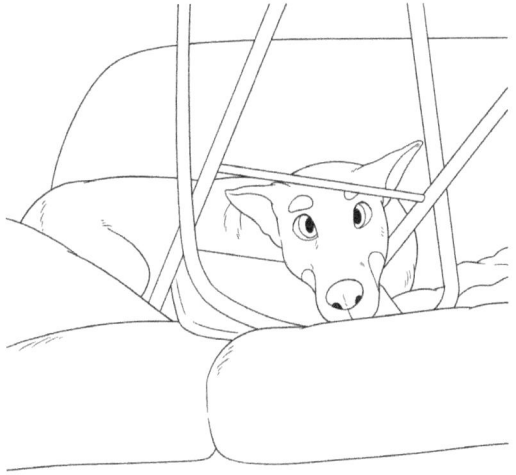

- His eyes would shoot open at the sound of the door.

- He would not even twitch. Only his eyes moved as he watched Dad pass through the living room.

- Once Dad was gone, Rumble would slowly stand, arch his back, stretch his legs, then shift his stiff body out from between the chairs, and creep to the floor with a disgruntled groan. It was brilliant!

I admired his stubborn determination. Rumble knew what he wanted and never stopped pursuing it. Even today, I think of him when I get discouraged. Whether I'm running down a dream or just enjoying a comfy nap, he taught me a great life lesson!

Paw-some Thought:

What have you always wanted
to pursue? Can you chase it with
dogged determination; doing one
thing every day to move you closer
to making it come true? Remember your "why." If something really
matters, you will figure out how
to make it happen.

Inspiring Quote:

It is impossible to forget a dog that gave you so much to remember.

~ IHEARTDOGS

Bible Verse:

In all labor there is profit, but idle chatter leads only to poverty.

PROVERBS 14:23

Silly Sally Sue

(Looking Back with Perspective)

Heaven goes by favor. If it went
by merit, you would stay out
and your dog would go in.

~ MARK TWAIN

Silly Sally (previously known as 'Thank You for the Music') turned ten years old and was due for her annual exam. A couple of weeks before, upon coming home from the groomer, we saw a lump on her right back leg, a few inches above her paw. It had been hidden in her fluffy fur but now the egg-sized lump was obvious. We brought it to the veterinarian's attention, and she took a sample for the lab.

We got the results back the following week and our fears were confirmed. Thankfully, it was not an aggressive form of cancer, but we were told the tumor would get bigger. According to the vet, even if the leg was amputated, the cancer might surface in another area of her body. The tumor was entwined with the tendons in her leg and there was no way to completely remove it so putting her through surgery, only to have it come back, did not make sense. Nor did we want to subject her to an amputation at that age. The vet agreed. As long as the tumor didn't bother her, we would move on with life as usual.

That was easier said than done. We shed some tears that night. The two years since Sally arrived had been such a joy. But then I considered all ten of her years. She was bred to be a show dog, and although her time in the spotlight was brief, I am sure it was glamorous. Then this beautiful former showgirl went on to have a few litters of future superstars before retiring in this lap of luxury. Leisurely morning naps with her head in the toy box, afternoons on long walks down tree-lined trails, and evenings curled up next to Josh while we watched TV. Who could ask for more?

But there was more. She accompanied us on doggie vacations to Taos, New Mexico, and Golden, and Woodland Park, Colorado, where we hiked, picnicked, and explored new grassy fields. And she learned the art of nose work. What a challenge that was. She didn't seem to have any idea what that big schnoz on her face was good for!

Ten years is certainly not young for an Airedale Terrier, but you wouldn't know it to meet the Sally Monster. She still prances around the house like she's hot-stuff, dashes around the backyard telling all the neighbors what was for dinner and digs under the house to lay in the cool dirt (so undignified)!

It is amazing how much life this dog packed into ten years. We will enjoy whatever time we have left with her and be thankful that we got to be just a little part of this sweet, sassy, silly pup's story.

Paw-some Thought:

We would not appreciate the thrill of victory if we never knew the misery of defeat. Life rarely feels balanced, but isn't it a grand journey?

Inspiring Quote:

This is a brief life, but in its brevity, it offers some splendid moments, some meaningful adventures.

~ UNKNOWN

Bible Verses:

Count it all joy when you fall into various trials, knowing that the testing of your faith produces patience. But let patience have its perfect work, that you may be perfect and complete, lacking nothing.

JAMES 1:2-4

So teach us to number our days, that we may gain a heart of wisdom.

PSALMS 90:12

Wyatt the Wonder Pug

(Wondering Why)

Dogs got personality.
Personality goes a long way.

~ QUENTIN TARANTINO

There were many dogs: big, bigger, small, tiny, skinny, stout, loud, and quiet. Then, in the last aisle of the kennels, our eyes met.

"Hello handsome," I offered as the robust twenty-five-pound pug waddled over.

The very alert matchmaker immediately suggested that we "meet." I was reluctant. I had come for a boxer, not a pug. I was so determined to get a boxer I had already promised myself that if one was not available that day, I would come back next weekend.

But heck, if this got the pug a little fresh air, why not? She put him on a leash, and we walked outside. He was well-mannered and affectionate, wanting to play and be pet. That smooshy face was irresistible. We lingered in the shade of a tree. I sat down with my back against the trunk, and he settled into my lap, as if this was a well-worn routine between us.

Meanwhile, the matchmaker looked up his background information. When we returned, she told me the pug had been surrendered only a couple of days before. I didn't care if he had been there for a year. In those ten brief minutes, I was hooked.

We got along famously. Early on, I noticed Wyatt had a bit of a stubborn streak. Having been told that I can occasionally be a tad obstinate, I could respect that. He was a clown. Who doesn't enjoy a good sense of humor? And he loved to eat. We were kindred spirits. Wyatt and I were soon inseparable.

Then, the picture-taking started: at the park, by the lake, napping, playing, close-ups, long-shots, etc. I sent one into the local newspaper in response to their Pet of the Week contest. We won (of course). They did a half-page write-up with a photo of Wyatt.

A week later, I received a call from the reporter.

She said she needed to tell me about something that she had never experienced in her decade-long career. A reader had recognized the pug as their dog, who had recently been surrendered to the Humane Society. Having read the article, the former owners were relieved to know the dog had been adopted into a loving home. They asked the reporter if she could find out if I wanted puppy pictures of Wyatt so I could have a complete portrait of his life. I did! More than that, I wanted to know them. I took their information and reached out.

We arranged a time to visit, and I learned their very sad story. The wife was being treated for an illness that, as it became worse, required hospitalization. The bills became overwhelming, and they could no longer afford their apartment. They moved in with her parents, who were allergic to dogs.

When the husband arrived at the Humane Society to surrender Wyatt, he learned that the shelter was full. The thought that his beloved pet might be euthanized was overwhelming. In a panic, he walked out with Wyatt still in tow. They paced outside the shelter as the man struggled with his decision. He was so distraught with worry that he stood within a couple feet of the shelter entrance, with Wyatt in his arms, pleading with each patron who approached to please take his dog.

The couple said it was the most heart-breaking season in their lives, and I believe it. We were all in tears as they described their sadness over losing him.

I've heard people wonder aloud how anyone could give up their dog. Often, it is because they do not have a choice. This is one of many sad examples, and yet there was still good that came out of it. My life would not have been nearly as complete without Wyatt in it.

Paw-some Thought:

Timing—is it everything or is it random? Discovering Wyatt was not a coincidence. It was a blessing that started a chain of shelter dog love stories that I hope never ends.

Lean into each season, whatever it brings. And rely on God's provision. You are here, now, for a time such as this.

Inspiring Quote:

Money can buy you a
fine dog but only love can
make him wag his tail.

~ KINKY FRIEDMAN

Bible Verse:

And God is able to make all grace abound toward you, that you, always having all sufficiency in all things, may have an abundance for every good work.

2 Corinthians 9:8

The Biggest Dog in the House

Some of my best leading men have been dogs and horses.

~ Elizabeth Taylor

It was my day off from the Humane Society, but I was there anyway. There were only two dogs living under our roof, which usually housed three. We needed to correct that void. An online search that Saturday morning indicated a senior beagle was waiting to be adopted. Although Josh and I arrived when the shelter opened, the line was already a dozen deep. We put our last name on the list and sat down.

Amazingly, we did not wait long. Around the corner came a long-haired chihuahua, followed by

Sheri, his walker, who was show-casing him. He teetered right over to us, so I sat on the floor to meet him. He crawled up into my lap and plopped down, like he had been waiting all morning for me to arrive. It made Sheri laugh.

"Isn't he cute?" she asked.

"Yes," I couldn't deny it, "What's his story?"

"He was a stray out at Red Rocks Open Space. Some hikers picked him up."

"A stray out there? We have rabbits in our back-yard bigger than him! How did he survive the coyotes, bobcats . . . even the hawks?"

Sheri was already shaking her head, "I wondered that too. All ten pounds of him."

I looked over at Josh who was shaking his head. We had come for a beagle, not this . . . this . . . Could he even be considered a dog? He more closely resembled a cat.

Reggie stirred, hopped out of my lap, and headed to Josh. (He had already won over one sucker, now on to conquer number two!) When Josh picked him up, Reggie rolled over, belly-up, and laid like a baby in Josh's arms, looking up with loving eyes.

Sheri continued Reggie's story, "We estimate that he is about ten years old. He came in two months ago with some significant health issues. All his teeth were rotten and had to be extracted."

Sheri handed us a five-page printout of medical notes. We stopped scanning half-way down the first page. Reggie had been neutered the same day all his teeth were pulled.

"Ohhh," Josh pointed at the note and cringed, "that had to be a rough day."

He held Reggie a little closer.

The rest, as they say, is history. We had come for a beagle, but it was Reggie who went home with us.

He had received a bit more food than necessary for his frame and with daily exercise, our little guy got even smaller. Weighing in at five pounds, he is the smallest dog we have ever had the honor of keeping. But don't be fooled by his size—the Regginator will always be the biggest dog in the house!

Confession

I did not want to be a matchmaker. When I attended Volunteer Info Night, I signed up to be a dog walker. I was approached by Claire, one of the coordinators, who told me that the real need at the time was for matchmakers.

But I had a good reason for wanting to walk dogs. In my line of work, I'm engaged with people ALL DAY LONG. Listening and talking. Talking and listening. Partnering to solve problems is rewarding, but by the time I get home, I don't want to make any decisions, even on what to eat for dinner.

Walking dogs was going to be a treat. Fresh air and belly rubs.

But I had to consider Claire's request. After all, I was there to help. If what they needed most was support in an area in which I was skilled, it seemed rather selfish not to do it.

I took a matchmaking shift once a week. Had I not made that commitment, none of these stories (or many other special experiences) would have been possible.

That volunteer job led to becoming a transport partner, and more adventure-filled stories. I am so thankful it worked out as it did. You never know where life will take you when you approach it with a prayer and an open heart. After all, why say 'no,' when saying 'yes' feels so good?

Princess Zoey

Sir Reginald
Poindexter
Alfieri III

Screamin' Dean

Sweet Lady Jane

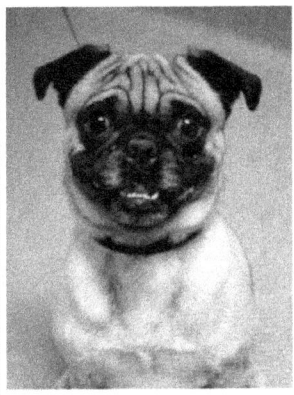

Mister Magoo

Silly Sally

The biggest dog
in the house

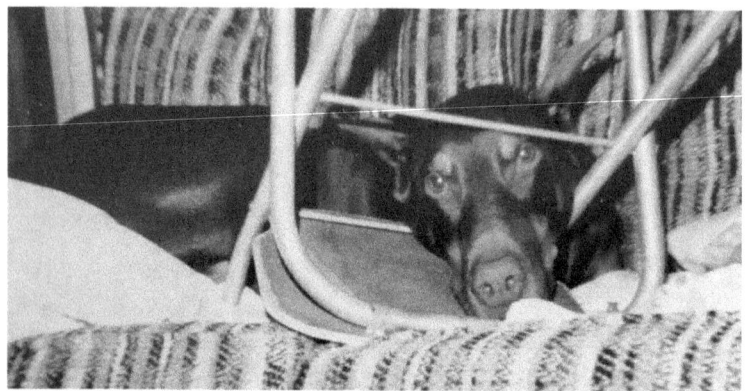

Rumble Rick

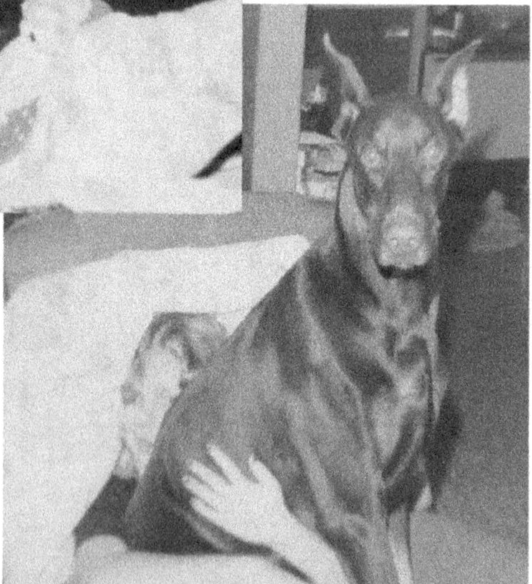

🐾
🐾
🐾
🐾
🐾
Duke
⬇️

My Copilot - Wyatt

Chance & Wyatt

Gratitudes

Thank you, to my first readers, for asking questions and providing valuable feedback.

- Patricia—for your sharp eye and thoughtful commentary.
- Neighbor Pat—for your joyful encouragement.
- Cori—for excusing the fact that there were no cats and critiquing it anyway.
- Erina—for being a fellow fanatic of words and storylines.

And to Pete and Joanne—for walking with me down the windy road to the paws-itively perfect title and cover illustration.

Thank you, to these Humane Society of the Pikes Peak Region (HSPPR) leaders for providing a review and endorsement:

- Duane Adams—Chief Executive Officer, HSPPR
- Julie Justman—Vice President of Operations, HSPPR
- Kelley Likes—Vice President of Philanthropy, HSPPR
- Jamie Norris—Director of Animal Law Enforcement, HSPPR

About the Author

When Jean's eyes locked with those of a smooshy-faced little dog who sat inside a kennel at the Humane Society, it was love at first sight. He captured her heart, and she captured their many adventures in short story poems for kids, starring *Zuggy the Rescue Pug*.

Jean is the leader of people engagement at the Pikes Peak Humane Society by day and a writer by night. She loves to touch readers' hearts with delightful stories about her canine companions. She and her husband are advocates for the adoption of senior dogs, or as they like to call them, 'vintage puppies.' They currently live in Colorado with their three fur kids and joke that although the humans pay the mortgage, it is really the dogs' house!

Would you like Jean to come and speak at one of your events? Be sure to book early. Jean has limited availability for speaking engagements, church programs, and school visits. Find out more @ JeanAlfieri or @ZuggythePug. Follow her on Facebook, YouTube and Instagram.